# UNDER HIS WING

ADVENTURES IN TRUSTING GOD

# UNDER HIS WING

## BERNIE MAY

Wycliffe
BIBLE TRANSLATORS
PO Box 628200
Orlando, Florida
32862-8200

Cover design and illustration by Britt Taylor Collins
Background photo by Forrest Zander
Back cover photo by Don Hesse

Inside photography by David Singer (pages xxxxx) and Britt Taylor Collins (page xx).

© 1979, 1983 by Multnomah Press, Portland, Oregon
Printed in the United States of America

Copyright assigned to Wycliffe Bible Translators, Inc.

Sixth Printing 2001

Library of Congress Cataloging in Publication Data

May, Bernie.
    Under His Wing

    Rev. ed. of: Climbing on course.
    1. Trust in God—Meditations. 2. May, Bernie.
1. Title.
BV4637.M36     242     82-24561
ISBN 0-930014-94-4

# Dedication

To my wife, Nancy, who today completes 38 years as copilot. Thanks for

holding the light,
checking the gauges,
correcting my heading,
caring for the passengers,
and helping me hold it on course.

Bernie May
5 June 1991

# Acknowledgement

God did a good thing when he put together as friends a pilot-sometime-writer (myself) with a writer-sometime-pilot. To Jamie Buckingham my sincere thanks for all his love, encouragement, and editorial help.

# Foreword

I highly commend to you the writings of Bernie May, missionary jungle pilot and humble servant of God. Bernie brings to these pages an unusual ability to turn the aviator's commonplace into spiritually exciting lessons.

Whether or not you've ever flown, you'll find you've been there too. As Bernie says, truth is for pilots and pilgrims alike. You will see yourself in these pages. Bernie's factual anecdotes, honest judgments, and sensitive application of scriptural truth will make you chuckle delightedly, sigh over shared foibles, and nod with approval when he decides God knows best how to keep us climbing on course.

I have long been interested in the ministry of Jungle Aviation and Radio Service (JAARS) and the organization it serves, Wycliffe Bible Translators. These intrepid servants of God are quietly and carefully reaching the unreachable with the precious Word of God in some of the most remote areas of the globe. For many years Bernie has been part of that very effective team. It's from that background he shares—simply and effectively.

Read. Be blessed. And keep *Under His Wing!*

Billy Graham

# Introduction

It's hard to tell whether I've learned more about flying from my time with God, or more about God from my experiences in an airplane. One thing is certain, however. During my thirty years as a missionary pilot, I have discovered the validity of certain biblical principles— principles concerning forgiveness, compassion, obedience, justice, and faith.

Especially faith!

All this came to mind recently when I took off from Long Beach Airport. Usually when I take off from Long Beach I can see for miles. In the harbor below is the Queen Mary resting at her berth. Off to one side is the city of Los Angeles, stretching down the coast. Circling back, I can see the Sierra Madre Mountains looming up on the horizon.

This Saturday was different. The weather was overcast. Visibility was less than a mile with smog and haze. Seconds after my wheels left the runway, I could no longer see the ground. I was on instruments. But after years of flying—including hundreds of hours on instruments—it was second nature to switch my gaze from the actual horizon outside to the instrument panel, and continue on as usual.

It hadn't always been that easy, though. I remember the first time I flew into the clouds. Suddenly, instead of being able to line up my wings with the green earth below and fix the nose of my plane on the horizon ahead, I had to rely on those little dials and gauges in front of me. It was scary. Instinct said to throttle back and feel my way through the clouds. How did I know what was in that cloud? Maybe a brick wall. What a relief when I burst out on the other side! All I had had to do was follow the instruments, take directions from the air traffic controller, and soon I was back in sunshine.

But Saturday morning as I took off from Long Beach, I was totally relaxed. Hundreds of hours in the clouds had taught me there was nothing to fear. There were no big solid lumps to clobber me, no quick bends in the road which would cause me to wind up in the ditch. That morning, even though I could see nothing, it made no difference. Instrument flying had become second nature. I simply climbed to my designated altitude, put the plane on automatic pilot, and pulled out my lunch. I enjoyed the ride through the clouds, even though down below the earth was in a dense fog.

I had learned to trust.

That is the reason I have written this book: To share some of these truths. As much as we enjoy living in the sunshine, most of life is on instruments. We seldom get to see what lies ahead. If we get to our destination, it will have to be by faith alone. And that's scary. Sure, we want to throttle back, grip the wheel with white knuckles, grit our teeth, and expect to run into something. But faith says Jesus has gone ahead. We have nothing to fear.

I have discovered that while walking by sight is desirable, walking by faith is exciting. That's what this book is: a collection of exciting little stories (most of which have to do with lessons I learned in the air) that will teach you how to live by faith.

Especially on cloudy days.

Bernie May

# Table of Contents

## Necessary Inspections

## Involvement with the Flight Plan

# REALITY AS SEEN
# FROM ABOVE

# The Million Dollar Simulator

The other day a lady asked if I had ever flown a jumbo jet—one of those huge birds that holds 400 passengers in its metal gullet. I almost said, "Yes," but had to limit my answer to, "Well, almost."

How do you almost fly a jumbo jet?

My good friend Roy Long, a senior pilot with a large commercial airline, is in charge of a jet pilot training program in Miami. Pilots preparing to fly the company's mammoth airships get their initial checkout in what is called a "simulator." It's an awesome-looking piece of machinery which contains a simulated jumbo-jet cockpit. Housed in a multi-million dollar training center, it stands on tall mechanical stilts which move a few feet back and forth—up and down—controlled by a roomful of computers.

One night Roy invited me to join in a training session. While the regular pilots were taking a coffee break, he gestured toward the simulator.

"Strap yourself in the left seat, Bernie, and let's make a couple of takeoffs and landings."

While I buckled up, Roy punched a few buttons on the console and somewhere a few rooms over, a metallic brain clicked and whirled in response and went right to work.

We found ourselves on the end of Runway 9-Left at Miami International. The computer left nothing to the imagination. I'd never been in such a high cockpit in my life. There was the Miami runway stretching out in front of me—glaring white in the mid-morning sun. I advanced throttle, heard the engines go from throaty rumble to mechanical scream, spooling up to max RPM. My jumbo started to roll forward as a stewardess somewhere back greeted the passengers. Beads of sweat formed on my brow while the runway flashed under me. The airspeed indicator crept past 140 KTS and Roy called out, "Rotate!"

I eased back the yoke. We were airborne—climbing into the hazy blue over Miami. In the weight of the controls, I could feel the huge craft behind me. *Sure would hate to land this bird in the Andes.* We climbed to pattern altitude. My copilot nodded as I circled the great field and lined up on final for the landing. Roy was calling out airspeed as I worked the throttles and controls—letting down for landing. I heard the wheels screech a protest on the runway and then felt the weight of the plane settle on the gear. My feet were on the brakes as I reversed the engines. We coasted to a shuddering halt.

"Not bad, Captain," Roy grinned. "Not bad at all for your very first landing in the L-1011." Running my sleeve across my brow, I was warmed by a feeling of accomplishment. No hitches or hang-ups. It felt good.

*But it wasn't real.* It was all a Disneyland make-believe. We hadn't traveled two feet. We never went higher than our stilts.

And that, I am slowly realizing, is a parable of much of our Christian experience. We build million-dollar simulators. We climb in, sing passionate hymns with an electronic organ that simulates 20 different instruments. We listen to exciting stories and even make emotional commitments. There's only one minor fraud. We never really take off. There is noise and motion—but we haven't gone anywhere.

"Spectator Christianity" has vaccinated us against the genuine article—participation Christianity. One church advertises, "For those who want more than a Sunday religion." Now, that's the way it should be.

Dr. Samuel Shoemaker asks us all, "What has Jesus Christ meant to you since 7:00 this morning? Is your Christianity ancient history or current events?"

God's invitation is to mount up with wings as eagles. Why be content with a simulator when you can fly?

# Hidden Wings

A friend of mine knows an airline captain who flies overseas routes for a U.S. carrier. Between trips to Europe and the Middle East, he runs a small filling station in the suburbs near his home. He gets a kick out of changing plugs and points and talking to the folks while he pumps gas.

One Saturday morning, dressed in his greasy overalls, he walked down to the local hardware store to pick up a wrench.

"What's new?" the store owner asked as he rang up the purchase.

"Ah, I'm thinking of taking the Cairo run this month," the captain said. "I enjoy flying to London and Frankfurt, but I think the change of pace will do me good."

He paid for the wrench and left.

Another customer, curious, asked, "Who's the world traveler?"

Rolling his eyes, the store owner nodded toward the departing pump jockey. "Some nut who runs the gas station down the street. Thinks he's an airline pilot!"

Both men got a good laugh out of that one.

It's easy to be deceived. I keep reminding myself of that when I see our JAARS people coming home on furlough. Arriving here at our JAARS Center in North Carolina, they look like ordinary people—a school teacher, a local farmer, an insurance salesman from Charlotte...or even a filling station operator. Who would dream that just a few days before, these same people were risking their lives flying a tiny airplane over the Amazon jungle, sending life-saving radio messages over the jigsaw islands of the Philippines, or rebuilding a damaged aircraft in the shadow of the Andes?

On the other hand, I was in the grocery store the other day and this ordinary-looking young man kept telling me about his Father, the King.

You never know, do you?

# What Counts Most?

It was 10:22 Tuesday morning, January 22, and the weather was sour, plus. I was over Sioux City, Iowa, in a Cessna 182 amphibian flying from Iquitos, Peru, to Winnipeg, Canada. It was snowing and the temperature was 20 degrees below.

The radios were on the blink, the engine was running rough, and the landing gear had frozen. One wheel was up, one wheel down. I was running out of airspeed, altitude, and experience all at once. Even though I was praying up there in the cockpit, I wished there were some way to let others know of my situation. I desperately needed their prayers, too.

As I let down through the snow to the Sioux City airport I realized I was going to have to land in a 30 knot quartering head wind. But it was God's provision. The wind was strong enough to allow me to land on one wheel and keep the other side in the air until I slowed and settled to the runway without a scratch. The asbestos-suited firemen didn't have to lift a finger. The plane was towed into a hangar, serviced, and the next day I completed the trip to Canada.

The following week I was in Colmar, Pennsylvania, and met a Mrs. Ziegler. She surprised me by saying that I was one of the missionaries for whom she often prayed.

"In fact," she said, "last Tuesday morning I was to attend a women's prayer meeting, but it was cancelled because of a snow storm. So I stayed home and spent half an hour in prayer just for you." We compared Sioux City time with Colmar time. At 10:22, this dear friend was kneeling before the throne, interceding for me. Right on!

On my office wall is a planning chart. It lists the men assigned to JAARS operations in 13 countries. Recently I've been taking a few minutes each day and praying for some of the people on that list. Each day I take a country, such as Bolivia, and spend a few minutes visualizing each man and his family. I try to visualize their circumstances, and then I ask God to meet their needs.

I do a lot of things for JAARS: planning, scheduling, managing, traveling, speaking, directing. Yet I'm slowly realizing that it is what God does for us that counts most. Who knows? Perhaps those few minutes that I spend in prayer each day are my most significant contribution.

It's not an idle statement. "More things are wrought by prayer than this world dreams of."

# Of Eagles and Turkeys

Recently a little saying has been making the rounds. It goes: "It's difficult to soar with eagles when you work with turkeys."

I've been wondering what would happen if a baby eagle were to get dropped in the turkey pen by mistake. It would grow up knowing nothing but turkey talk and turkey walk. Even though it didn't look like a turkey, the rest of the birds would do everything possible to convince him he was one of them. He might even learn to gobble.

But inside, he would never be a turkey. He would always be restless. And when the day came that he saw another eagle, his wings outstretched, riding the thermals above the mountains, he would know. Spreading his wings, he would do the thing a turkey would never dare: he would fly. He would soar. And he would never return to the squalor of the turkey pen.

When faced with God's truth, we must either go up to where God is—or bring God down to our turkey pen.

Unfortunately, many of us spend our time attempting to do the latter; trying to justify our turkey actions when God is calling us to forsake the pen for the heights.

Religion is my response to the God I know. If my concept of God is limited, my response will be limited. If I see God as a person, I will be content to gobble—not soar.

What does all this mean when you're out on the mission field—struggling each day with unfamiliar words in a translation, battling heat, insects, rash and not enough money to put gasoline in your motor scooter? What does it mean when you get a letter that a church you long counted on has dropped your support, or a doctor brings a report that a loved one is gravely ill?

What does it mean on the homefront? When the bills are piling up at the house and the job market is limited; or the kids are not getting along and you and your wife don't have enough time together any more; or your work sits in mounds at home and at the office, and you can't feel beyond the day-to-day struggles to a fresh breath of air from the Lord?

It means you keep reminding yourself who you are in Christ. And you remind your brother and sister, who may be dragging their own tail feathers through the turkey yard, who they are, too.

A friend sometimes winds up his conversation by saying, "Keep looking down!"

I didn't understand what he meant until I ran across that verse where Paul reminds us we are seated with Christ in heavenly places.

Turkeys look up, and yearn.

Eagles soar with God, looking down on an earth which is God's footstool—not Satan's domain.

Don't forget who you are. Even though you may be far away.

# GUIDED BY THE PILOT

# Holding Pattern

The September heat marbled the air off the concrete apron as we taxied away from the terminal building in Richmond, Virginia. Jamie Buckingham, his lap full of charts, was beside me in the right seat. Bill Sasnett was in the rear, mopping his face with a handkerchief.

We were bound in our Helio Courier for New York City. Before leaving the terminal I had filed a flight plan with the FAA, requesting a direct route. In the jungle I feel comfortable flying the little Helio. But this was urban America, and at 120 mph I wanted to spend as little time as possible competing with jumbo jets around New York City.

Now, sitting at the end of the runway, I finished the run up. Mags, prop, generator, instruments—all okay. The cabin was like a furnace as we waited for clearance. We wanted to hear those three sweet words, "Cleared as filed," and get on our way up and out of the heat.

Finally the radio crackled to life. "Helio Courier 242 Bravo, are you ready to copy your clearance?"

I could tell by the voice from the tower that we weren't going to get our direct route. Instead, we were directed to turn southeast after takeoff and climb to 3,000 feet—not the 7,000 I had requested. Then another controller gave us various headings which took us east toward Chesapeake Bay. We were then directed to climb to 5,000 feet, through turbulent air, zigzag over three different airways, and finally head west. All this, to get us on the NYC airway which ran north.

It was aggravating, but the Air Traffic Control fellows have to take a lot of things into account. We weren't the only ones in the air. In fact, the NYC controller said he had 70 planes on his radar scope. Besides this, there were thunderheads which easily could have torn the wings off our plane.

We didn't get what we asked for. Instead, we got what was best for us—and best for everyone else, too.

Holding patterns, turbulent air, going east when you want to go north—all seem confusing. But when somebody who knows the way and the obstacles is plotting your path, you accept his instructions gladly.

Proverbs 14:12 tells us:

> There is a way which seems right to a man,
> But its end is the way of death.

The ways of God may seem to defy our reasoning. But He knows the end from the beginning. In the long run, God's skies are always friendly skies. Even when you're in a holding pattern.

# Letting the PILOT Pilot

The wheels of the heavily loaded Cessna 206 had barely left the wet jungle airstrip. The pilot had the throttle pushed all the way to the firewall. He had done this many times before and was confident they would clear the huge trees.

Then, as nearly as we can tell, the passenger sitting next to him had a surge of panic. Glancing up, he saw the onrushing trees filling the windshield. Fearful they were going to crash, he tried to help. Apparently he took hold of the flight controls and pulled back. His assistance proved to be disastrous—almost fatal.

But his intentions were only the best. The fully loaded airplane wasn't climbing very rapidly in the hot jungle air.

Huge trees at the end of the strip were looming large.

*"My soul—what's wrong with that pilot? Is he asleep? Why doesn't he pull back on the controls?"*

But it doesn't work that way. You have to build up airspeed before you point the nose skyward. Otherwise you'll stall.

The airplane pitched up, lost critical airspeed, and began to settle toward the jungle below. The pilot wrenched the controls back and tried desperately to get the nose down. But it was too late. As the airplane reached stalling speed the heavy engine pulled the nose over sharply and the craft spun to earth.

By God's grace, no one was killed, but all were injured, the pilot most seriously. Another plane happened to be on the ground and its pilot rescued the injured, making two flights to get all to a small jungle hospital where they eventually recovered.

There are many people who find it difficult to keep their hands off the controls. And the crashes continue. I sympathize with the frightened passenger, for I have a way of doing exactly the same thing in my spiritual journey. Thinking God has lost control or has ceased to care, I panic and try to take over and run things my way. It never works. Even the Lord Jesus had to submit to His Father's flight plan.

*Not My will, but Yours be done.*

Things may seem mighty awkward—or even scary—but we have to be willing to leave the controls in the hands of the Pilot.

It's the only way to fly.

# A Voice in the Storm

The controller's voice from Houston Center was calm.

"We understand," he said. "One engine has failed. We have you on radar. Montgomery County Airport is 45 minutes southeast of your position. Would you like vectors?"

For the last half hour I had been enjoying the bright Texas sky as we cruised high above an overcast. Below us, rain and fog blanketed the ground between Dallas and our destination, Houston. Then, BANG! One engine on the Cessna sputtered and stopped. The dead prop on my right looked strange and ominous. I could still fly—one of the joys of twin engines—but I was not overly ecstatic about making a single-engine approach into an unknown airport in weather that had the ducks walking.

I glanced over at my two passengers. They were staring, transfixed, at the motionless propeller.

"We'll soon be on the ground at another airport," I said, in a weak effort to allay their anxieties. But who was around to comfort me? I reached for the mike and soon the reassuring voice of the Houston controller filled the cabin.

"Okay, Houston," I responded, "I'm with you. Requesting vectors to Montgomery Airport."

"Turn left," he said. "Heading 110 degrees. Descend to 4,000 feet."

I followed his directions implicitly, trying to keep the airplane trim and level at the same time. At 4,000 we entered the clouds, flying blind through the mist and rain.

"Descend to 3,000 and turn right five degrees," the steady voice instructed.

"Descend to 2,000 and turn left five degrees...Now turn right 30 degrees and descend to 1,500 feet."

As we dipped into the rainclouds, I could barely see the tip of my wing. But I knew he knew where I was. That was enough. I didn't know his name. I had never seen his face. But I knew I could trust him. I had no other choice—unless I wanted to try and make it on my own.

Suddenly we broke out of the clouds and there it was: a mile of wet asphalt glistening in the rain. I'd never known asphalt to look so beautiful.

I'd been more than willing to entrust my life to a faceless voice speaking complex directions through the fog. Touching down, I thought of another voice. Calm, patient, ever present when over the years blinding mists have thrown carefully wrought plans into chaos. His voice.

Did I really trust that voice? As much as I trusted the stranger in Houston? Would I be willing to follow exacting instructions when I couldn't see any farther than the end of my nose?

Good questions. Questions which have to be answered...on a regular basis...like every morning.

*Though you have not seen him, you love him; and even though you do not see him now, you believe in him and are filled with an inexpressible and glorious joy* (I Peter 1:8 NIV).

# A Question of Focus

One of the most difficult lessons to teach new pilots about landing on short, hazardous airstrips is to keep their eyes on the good part of the strip, rather than on the hazard. The natural tendency is to concentrate on the obstacle, the danger, that thing he is trying to avoid. But experience teaches us that a pilot who keeps his eye on the hazard will sooner or later hit it dead center.

If he keeps looking at the ditch at the side of the strip, inevitably he will run into it. If he focuses on the stump near the roll-out area, he'll likely bang his prop against it. The experienced pilot focuses his attention solidly on the track he wants the plane to follow, keeping the hazards in his peripheral vision only.

Pilots aren't the only ones who wrestle with this problem of focus. Anyone who majors on minors, who constantly talks about his problems, who always fears the worst, or habitually points out reasons why a plan of action won't work, will get precisely what he is trying to avoid. The Bible says a man is what he thinks. And poor Job indicated what he had been thinking about all along when he said, "For the thing which I greatly feared is come upon me."

Take demons and evil spirits.

They're very real hazards. But get overconcerned about them and pretty soon they'll be all over you like a swarm of bees. The wise man focuses on Jesus Christ.

And what about those dangerous doctrinal differences looming up at the end of the strip as you try to take off?

Concentrate on division and you'll wind up in the middle of a split. But focus on unity, on the things that unite rather than the things that divide, and you'll clear those obstacles with room to spare.

On my first assignment as a JAARS pilot in Peru, I was dispatched to fly three businessmen to a mountain town high in the Andes. The men had previously flown with some of our older, more experienced pilots, and were apprehensive about being piloted by a 22-year-old who was busy plotting his course on a wrinkled old map.

As I loaded their baggage, they stood to one side, talking in anxious tones. Finally one of them asked, "Captain, how long have you flown in Peru?"

"About a year," I answered.

They were increasingly nervous.

"Captain, are you sure you know where all the mountain ridges and peaks are between here and Tingo Maria?"

"No, sir," I answered. "But I know where they're not. And that's the course we're going to fly."

They looked at each other, smiled, and climbed aboard.

There are many dangers on each side. But Jesus has gone before and prepared the way. I know it sounds simplistic, but all we have to do is focus on Him and pretty soon we'll be wheels up, and climbing on course.

# TRUSTING HIS CONTROL

# Practice Makes Permanent

I never did like to play on the black keys. As a kid, it became such an issue to me that I quit piano lessons. I'd do it my own way. And for years, every time I sat down at the piano I played only on the "preferred" keys—the white ones. Finally, a few years back, I decided to take lessons again. After six months *my teacher* quit. It was no use. "My way" was so ingrained I could not break the old habit and do it correctly. The "black key syndrome" haunts me to this day.

It reminds me of something my colleague Merrill Piper says in his flight safety seminars. "Practice does not make perfect," says Merrill. *"Practice makes permanent."*

The principle has drifted back to bedevil our ministry again and again. Recently one of our pilots was practicing emergency power-off landings. We teach that this should be done with the engine idling. But this pilot shut it off completely. When the heavy plane began settling far more rapidly than expected, he attempted a quick restart. It didn't work. The plane crashed, injuring the pilot and damaging the aircraft.

"Where did he ever get the idea to kill the engine?" I asked Merrill as we reviewed the accident report. "He should have known better. Why did he do it?"

"Unfortunately," Merrill explained, "his instructors in basic training taught him to make practice landings that way. Even in advanced training this was accepted procedure. Later, they recognized that it was dangerous."

But the change came after our man graduated. When he got into one of our heavier planes, his old habit flipped a switch in his head and off went the power. His practice almost made *him* permanent.

I'm amazed at how hard it is to change attitudes and opinions that we learn early. I have friends who learned in their youth that the Sermon on the Mount was just for the Jews, or that miracles ceased after the first century.

I wonder how many of my classmates crashed because they didn't expect a miracle. Up came the old prejudice and off went the power. Or perhaps they haven't clung to the sure and changeless footholds of our Lord's timeless mountain message. But I have. The rock-firm promises have never given way beneath my trembling feet and searching hands.

Clinging to God's powerful promises...that's one practice our Lord makes perfect *and* permanent.

# On the Promise of a Friend

He said it so casually.

"Bern, how would you like to take a trip with me around the world?"

My businessman friend Bill Johnson and I had been strolling down a hot, crowded street in Quito, Ecuador.

"Are you serious?" I asked, astonished. I'd done a lot of flying over the jungles of South America but a flight around the globe was only daydream stuff.

"Sure I'm serious. I love to travel and have always wanted to go around the world. Why don't you come with me?"

It was a little overwhelming. Around the world! But missionaries are not, as a rule, wealthy. Such a trip would cost several thousand dollars, and besides, I suspected Bill's tastes were rather more sophisticated than mine.

We chatted on, plotting the details. We would visit

Japan, Hong Kong, Taiwan, then our Wycliffe-JAARS program in the Philippines, down to Papua New Guinea and Australia, up to Indonesia, and over to Singapore. We would hit Southeast Asia and India, stopping at Tehran, Beirut, and Rome before coming home. The trip would take six weeks and, I could tell from my friend's animated expression, would cost a small fortune.

Finally I spoke up. "Uh, Bill..." I stuttered, breaking into the conversation, "this really sounds great but...."

Bill knew what I was thinking. Clapping me on the shoulder he said, "Now, Bern, don't worry about the expenses. I'll take care of everything—first class all the way!"

We hadn't even bought the tickets and I was already so excited I could hardly talk. I couldn't wait to get back home that evening and tell my wife. We talked into the night, thinking about all the mysterious, exotic places I would get to visit and explore.

However, that night as I laid my head on the pillow, a strange sense of conviction came over me. In the deep, quiet area of my life where God often speaks, I heard a silent voice.

"You're sure excited, aren't you, son?"

"Yeah, I guess I am."

There was a pause, then, "Do you realize why you are so excited, Bernie? It's because of the promise of a friend. The trip is still weeks away, but because you trust this man, you're acting as though it's already happened."

Another long pause. "How long has it been since you were that excited over My promises? Or...don't you trust Me as much as your friend Bill?"

I didn't sleep well that night. But the lesson was well-learned. And just as Bill's promise materialized and I was able to make that memorable journey, so I have discovered that all of God's promises are true. In fact, I can trust my Heavenly Father even more than the promises of all my friends.

Now that's something to get excited about!

# Overcontrolling

I can still hear my flight instructor of 20 years ago shouting above the engine noise of the Super Cub, "You're overcontrolling!"

He was right. As a beginning pilot, I was afraid if I didn't keep my feet firm on the rubber pedals and my fingers clenched tightly around the stick, the plane simply wouldn't stay in the air. I blush when I recall sitting in the cockpit, jaw muscles tight, stomach churning, flying all over the sky.

"Relax," my instructor grinned. "Ease off on the controls and the plane will fly itself."

That was good advice 20 years ago. It's even better advice today. The novice Christian develops ulcers because he's overcontrolling. The mature believer, however, has that relaxed look about him.

Even missionaries have discovered that it is possible to do the Lord's work without the Lord's power—but it will kill them in the process. However, when they let the source of power, the Holy Spirit, rule in their lives, they stop overcontrolling. White knuckles around the stick begin to relax. What used to be drudgery can become fun.

Those of us in JAARS have always had a certain pride in our professionalism. Yet our motto, "We do our best and the Lord does the rest," sometimes meant we thought we could handle most emergencies ourselves. If we couldn't, we would call on God.

Now many of us have come to realize that our best is not good enough. We used to throw around that phrase, "God is my copilot." No more. He's flying left seat—we are the copilot! The difference is, instead of giving God directions, we're taking orders from Him.

We find the power in the Spirit, not in our striving. Anyone can get uptight about tomorrow, and wander all over the sky today. The Spirit-filled man not only flies straight and level, but he's relaxed when he reaches his destination.

# Overboard!

A lady wrote to JAARS recently asking to be put on our mailing list for "that new publication." She wasn't sure of the name but she thought it might be "Overboard."

Not bad. The name of the publication may actually be *Beyond*, but the call of God *is* for His people to go "overboard" as He directs.

My wife, Nancy, thought I had gone over the edge the night a friend phoned from California. He said he knew where we could buy a $50,000 Helio Courier for $27,500. But we needed to act immediately.

We had a "new plane" account on our books, but it was $15.83 in the red. I ordered the plane anyway. No doubt about it—it was an "overboard" kind of thing to do. Not unlike Peter's decision—who suddenly crawled over the edge of his fishing boat, planted his feet solidly on a passing wave, and started striding. Today that plane is paid for, doing duty on the mission field.

Our plan to put seven helicopters in operation within three years also sounded a little overboard. We lacked the equipment, personnel, funds, and technical expertise for such a project. But we decided to go ahead anyway. Step by step, we experienced a series of miracles.

In a surplus depot in Pennsylvania, our man Jim Baptista spotted 16 metal engine containers used by the military to ship new engines. Since we'd been having trouble with our old wooden crates, Jim asked if we could have those metal ones. "You can have all 16," the man said. Looking closer, Jim discovered each container had inside it a spare engine, just the type used in our Hiller helicopters. Just like that God had supplied 16 spare helicopter engines!

Jim got more than he asked for—or even dreamed. Kind of reminds me how the apostle Paul liked to describe his Lord:

*Now to him who is able to do immeasurably*
*more than all we ask or imagine, according to*
*his power that is at work within us.*
That's overboard!

# Just Me, God, and the Night

There are occasional moments in life when God gets my absolute attention. Like when the engine quits on takeoff at 800 feet over a busy city. Or the fuel tank runs dry. Or ice forms on the wings faster than you can measure. Or you run out of runway and experience at the same time.

Recently I was taking off from Charlotte airport in a single engine Bellanca. It was a rainy, foggy night. Ceiling was 300 feet, visibility less than a mile. Departing Runway 5, the controller cleared me to 3,000 feet and told me to turn to a 180 degree heading. As I was climbing to altitude and turning south, the lights on the instrument panel suddenly went dim. I glanced at the amp meter. It was showing 45 amps discharge. The alternator had failed and I had lost all electrical power. Faintly, just before the radio faded out completely, I heard the controller say, "Seven Four Romeo you have just faded off my radar screen."

I quickly turned off everything electrical. I needed to save whatever juice there was left in the battery to lower my landing gear—presuming I ever found the airport in that soup.

I was alone in the darkness. No radio. No navigation signals. No lights. No contact with the ground. Lost in the rain and clouds over a busy airport.

My three passengers, dear friends, giants in the faith, loving associates—could not help me. I wasn't afraid. No child of God needs to fear, regardless how horrible the situation. No, it was a different kind of emotion. Loneliness. I was alone. Cut off from all I depended upon. Just me, God, and the darkness.

A friend of mine says God sends periods of loneliness to show us our true condition. When the props fall, the masks come off, all the supports give way—it is then we find out who we really are. And, more important, who He is.

There was enough battery left to get one radio working. I established contact with the tower, who vectored me back to Charlotte airport. By keeping the radio off most of the time, and using no lights, I was able to get the gear down and have enough juice left to use the ILS navigation.

We broke out of the clouds at 300 feet and there was that beautiful runway stretching before me.

Back on the ground I taxied to the hangar and cut the engine. There wasn't enough charge left in the battery to re-start. The short in the alternator had drained everything except what we needed to get back on the ground.

We praised the Lord and joked about the situation, but the reflections of that loneliness linger on. Perhaps we are made to be lonely. Maybe this is what Augustine had in mind when he made that statement about our souls being restless until they find their rest "in Thee."

I wonder if Augustine came up with that one on a rainy night after his alternator failed.

# Heading into the Wind

A brisk autumn wind stung my cheeks and swirled dry leaves into the air as we made our way across the plowed field toward the little airport. I had never seen an airplane up close and Dad had promised that come Saturday we would go out to the airport and see the big two-motor plane that landed there each afternoon. I don't remember how old I was, eight or nine I guess, but I'll never forget the excitement. I think my father was as excited as I.

The DC-3 was parked in front of the passenger building. We stood behind a fence and watched the half-dozen people climb aboard, holding on to their hats and leaning into the wind.

Dad and I talked about the wind. Could the plane take off in such strong gusts? Dad wasn't sure, but figured if the plane taxied down to the end of the field to take off with the wind to its tail, the breeze would undoubtedly push that big passenger ship into the air.

Much to our surprise, the plane rumbled out in the opposite direction and took off straight into the wind. Amazed, we craned our necks as it climbed over us and banked toward Philadelphia. We talked about it for days. It seemed incredible—taking off into the wind like that. Why do you suppose the pilot did that?

The idea that I would ever get to ride in such a plane, much less fly one, was a dream beyond hope. But in God's providence, I realized that dream and became a pilot on that grand old Douglas flying machine, the DC-3. I quickly learned its sensitivity to the wind. Not only in takeoffs and landings, but when taxiing on the ground.

One night, after landing in gale winds at Miami

International Airport, it took me 45 minutes to taxi from the runway to the terminal. If I turned sideways, the plane tried to tip up on its wing. Downwind I had no control at all. DC-3 pilots have learned, some to their embarrassment, that only when you head into the wind can you make the plane behave.

I've learned that in life, too. People going downwind never have control. They often wind up in ditches. And making turns can be disastrous. The only safe place in adversity is facing it head on. You may not make much progress—but at least you won't be flipped on your side, pushed off the edge of the runway, or wind up with a bent wingtip.

If we're ever going to reach our intended heights, we'll have to do it heading into the wind.

# THE CHARACTER OF GOD'S AIR BORN

# Broken Volunteers

A stewardess was handing out pillows in the plush, first-class cabin of a transcontinental airline. Pausing by a dignified lady in an aisle seat, the girl asked the passenger if she would like a pillow. The lady looked straight ahead, seemingly unaware of the stewardess.

The girl tried again—a little louder. **"Would you like a pillow, ma'am?"**

No response.

After a long pause, the lady's husband leaned over and said, "I'm sorry, Miss, but my wife never speaks directly to servants."

Ouch!

Needless to say, the "stew" was a bit stewed. Most in that lofty occupation don't think of themselves as servants. Yet, in reality, that's exactly what they are. They exist to *serve* the passengers.

Unfortunately, the word "servant" is also unpopular among Christians. We chafe at an order to carry someone's load that first mile—let alone the second. And the idea of washing someone else's feet is only two points above repulsive.

Even among missionaries I find a cool response to this title—servant. The word "volunteer" seems to fit our image better. But God isn't looking for volunteers. To volunteer implies that we make the terms. Some of us have gone out, egos waving from our lances, to "do a great work for God." The fortunate ones come back broken, realizing God doesn't need volunteers. He's simply looking for a few good men and women who will report for duty. Servants.

If God's Word is going to be translated into every

language in the world, it will only be accomplished through servants—servant translators, servant radio technicians, servant carpenters, servant pilots, servant secretaries. Servants who pray, servants who give, servant Christians everywhere.

And there's a bonus. Our Master talks directly to His servants. He even calls us friends.

# Mountain Wave Depression

Flying from New York to Washington in a twin-engine Beechcraft, I was tuned to Air Traffic Control when I heard a pilot report over Lancaster. He was on the same route, flying northbound at 7,000 feet, a thousand feet below me. In a shaky voice, he asked New York Center for clearance to land at Lancaster Airport.

"I can't maintain my altitude," he said.

New York cleared him to land at Lancaster and asked what was the problem.

"I really don't know," he replied. "I'm getting full RPM and manifold pressure but the airplane keeps sinking. I can't keep it in the air. Must have engine trouble." Then he switched frequencies and that's all I heard from him.

Twenty minutes later, as I approached Lancaster, *my* airplane started to settle. Airspeed dropped off from 160 knots to 110 knots. I increased power to climb settings. It still settled. Engine instruments checked okay, but I was fighting to hold the plane in the air. Then I remembered the other pilot had reported the same conditions. Weird!

As I struggled at the controls, something filtered back to me from my background reading. An expression.

*Mountain wave depression.* I had felt the effects of downdrafts in my mountain flying experience over the Andes of South America. But this was different. The winds were out of the west at 40 knots. I was just east of the Allegheny Mountains and the wind coming over the range was causing a huge depression area, not a momentary downdraft. It was like flying through a waterfall of wind.

Realizing this, I just stayed with it for the next 35 miles, fighting through the constant down pressures. Even with increased power I was barely able to hold the airplane in the air. Sooner or later, I believed I would break through.

Approaching Westminster, I suddenly started getting the reverse effects—*updrafts.* There was a tremendous, irresistible lift in the air. I reduced power 'way back, yet even so, my airspeed climbed over 200 knots and I could hardly keep the plane level. Risers were everywhere. I thought of that fellow on the ground back in Lancaster, nervously checking his engine. If only he had stayed with it a little longer, he would have passed beyond the influence of mountain wave depression.

Sound familiar? If you're like me, the analogy holds true for day-to-day living. I often find it difficult to hold a level course. The updrafts and downdrafts seem so unpredictable and sometimes come so close together. I'm encouraged by Paul, who had been through the depressions and then wrote back to say, "And let us not get tired of doing what is right, for after a while we will reap a harvest of blessing if we don't get discouraged and give up" (Galatians 6:9 TLB).

# Exit, the Swashbuckler

Humility comes hard for pilots. Even Christian pilots. There is something about getting behind the controls of a plane that makes a man feel, well, proud. The old caricature of the swaggering pilot with leather jacket, goggles, and scarf fits most of us more than we care to admit.

Spiritual pride—the kind that goeth before a fall—snares even the best. In fact, believing you are worthy to be counted among the best is sure evidence you've already fallen.

I keep remembering the smirk on the face of one of our Peru pilots when he sauntered into the hangar following a long, hard trip over the jungle. Dropping his flight bag, he boasted, "In four days I have traveled more miles than the apostle Paul in all his missionary journeys."

A seasoned missionary in the hangar never looked up from his packing as he replied: "Yes, but did you accomplish as much?"

Would you like to know an effective anti-toxin for a case of pride poisoning? Get yourself in a position where, if God doesn't take over, you're bound to fail. That was the way I felt when I started making plans to fly a new Cessna 402 across the Pacific to Papua New Guinea. Even having another experienced pilot like Ken Wiggers along as my copilot didn't ease the humble feelings I experienced every time I looked at those charts representing 8,000 miles of open sea. I immediately purchased two more books on prayer. When you file a flight plan from Oakland to Honolulu, you put "Glory" as your alternate destination.

By the time I was wheels up, I was all "prayed out." In fact, I was three weeks ahead in my devotions. This was one time I was determined to give God all the glory.

Just before we left I got a telegram from a good friend who's also a retired executive of Northrup Institute of Technology, my alma mater:

**AS YOU LEAVE THE SHORE LINE SATURDAY CONTINUING WEST COMMA I KNOW THAT OF THOSE FIFTY FOUR THOUSAND ANGELS OF MATTHEW TWENTY SIX FIFTY THREE COMMA EACH HAVING THE POWER SHOWN BY THE ONE IN SECOND KINGS NINETEEN THIRTY FIVE COMMA AT LEAST ONE HAS ORDERS TO FLY RIGHT WINGMAN WITH YOU AND AUTHORITY TO SUMMON A WHOLE FORMA-TION OR EVEN A SQUADRON ACCORDING TO WHAT MANEUVERS THE ENEMY MAKES PERIOD SO JUST WATCH YOUR LORAN AND REJOICE PERIOD PRAISE THE LORD**

And God performed miracles on that trip. The engines ran perfectly. Even with an extra ton of fuel, the Cessna soared over the waves like a tireless gull. And when we spotted Hawaii after seven hours of dead reckoning, most of it at night, Ken and I both shouted, "Praise the Lord!"

On the next leg we had to deal with five typhoons. At one point the Lord opened a hole in the clouds just in time for us to see an island whose radio beacon had blown down in the typhoon. The flyboys could call it skill if they wanted, but I say it was God's grace that got us there.

However, after we arrived in Papua New Guinea, a strange thing began to happen. I found myself enjoying all the congratulations, the "ohs" and the "ahs." Outwardly I was still giving God the credit, but inwardly I was accepting the praise and claiming it for myself. It's easy to get proud once you're safely on the ground.

But God had a way of dealing with that, too. The next morning I climbed into the right seat to check out one of the pilots who would fly the 402. Just seconds into the takeoff run the right engine failed. It stopped dead. I chopped power and hit the brakes. We aborted the take-off without incident and, using the one good engine, gingerly taxied back to the hangar. There the mechanic found that a part of the engine had seized, causing the failure.

I broke out in a cold sweat. Why had it run perfectly halfway around the world, only to fail just then? I don't know. But I do know this: It was time for the old swashbuckler to stash his scarf and goggles. From now on, God gets *all* the glory—in the air and on the ground.

# The People God Uses

It's strange, the people God uses.

A large church had invited me as their special guest so they could present an airplane as a gift to JAARS. It was a Bible-believing church, filled with scrubbed-faced fundamentalists—the kind I like to be around. I was the main speaker for the Sunday morning service—a real VIP.

During Sunday school a friend introduced me to a beautiful black woman who, learning I was to speak, was visiting the church for the first time. I immediately recognized her, although we had never met. She was Josephine Makil, a Wycliffe translator, home on furlough from Vietnam.

Some months before, she and her family had been ambushed on a lonely Vietnam road. She and three of her children had watched in horror as her husband, and the fourth child he was holding in his arms, were murdered in cold blood. She is one of God's special people.

That morning, before I spoke, I introduced Josephine, asking her and the children to stand. She gave a brief but powerful testimony, closing by saying, "I can testify that God's ways are perfect and His grace is sufficient."

The words burned deep in my heart. I wanted to remove my shoes, so hallowed was the ground as I stood beside her. It took me long moments before I could speak. I couldn't get the lump out of my throat.

After the service people flocked around me, shaking my hand and patting my back. During the adulation I happened to look to one side. There stood Josephine and the children. Alone. In fact, the people were deliberately avoiding her. She was black.

I could hardly restrain my anger. I wanted to rush through that magnificent building, overturning the pews and shouting, "Keep your money. Keep your handshakes. Keep your airplane. It goes up as a stench before God."

But I didn't. Perhaps I was too much the coward. I did break from the group and go to Josephine. We chatted, but she said nothing about her rejection. She reacted to those church people the same way she reacted to those who murdered her husband—with love and forgiveness.

These people found it strange that God would use a black person like Josephine. I, in turn, find it strange that God would use people like those in that church—yet their gift has been a blessing to the Kingdom.

But then, I am sure some folks find it strange that God would use a fellow like me.

Josephine is right. Love is the only way to react. For all our sakes, we must leave judgment to God.

# On Losing and Winning

The idea of "giving up" never appeals to us masculine types. We prefer the pull-yourself-up-by-your-bootstraps method, the blood-sweat-and-tears approach to life.

This brings to mind R. G. LeTourneau's little Piper Tri-Pacer. The incident occurred in the late 1950s on a jungle airstrip in the foothills of the Andes. There were four big men in the plane; it was a simple case of too much weight and not enough horsepower. Staggering off the end of the mountain strip, the Piper settled into the middle of a swirling jungle river, and flipped over.

The men quickly scrambled out of the plane and began swimming frantically toward shore, only 50 yards away. But the current was much too strong. Before they had fought 10 yards toward shore, they had been swept a quarter mile downstream. Death seemed imminent.

Totally exhausted, the first man finally gave up. But as his body went limp and his feet began to settle, they touched the bottom of the riverbed. To his amazement and joy, the river, which was sweeping them towards their death, *was only 30 inches deep*. Standing tall in the water he shouted to his struggling companions to stop swimming and put their feet down.

Rejoicing, but red-faced, all four men waded safely to shore.

I've done that so often it hurts to think about it. Only God knows how much my arms and legs ache from the futile exercise of trying to stay afloat in shallow water. It's like flying white-knuckled all through life.

Again and again I have been forced to give up. Each time my masculinity takes another blow. But each time the words of my Lord are stenciled on the back walls of my mind just that much clearer. It is possible to struggle doggedly and lose everything. It is also possible to lose your life and, in the process, really find it.

# The R & R Formula

Something happens to me when I lose my pen.
I become animalistic.

"All right, who stole my pen...? What do you mean 'you borrowed it'? You *stole* it...! That's the problem with you kids. No respect for other people's property."

I have probably learned more about myself in that two-minute period following the discovery that my pen is missing than at any other time in my life. And it is not very nice.

In that brief moment of supreme indignation I am fully able to justify divorce, brutality, mental cruelty, and even public ridicule. After all, how do you teach your wife and children proper standards of conduct if you don't take a stand on a thing? If a wife is capable of stealing a man's pen to write out a shopping list, where will she stop? What remains sacred?

A friend of mine has developed a rather intimidating formula to measure Christian maturity. Maturity, he says, can be measured by the time it takes to move from *Reaction* to *Recovery*.

He calls it the R & R Formula.

The next time someone steals your pen—or drives a nail through your hand—see how long it takes from Reaction to Recovery. It'll tell you something about yourself. I know people who are still reacting to things which happened 40 years ago. They've *never* recovered. Most likely, they never will.

"You are only young once," said a dry-witted sage, "but you can be immature for a lifetime."

Not long ago I had a good opportunity to put the R & R Formula through the acid test. Next to my pen, my most sacred possession is a well-worn pocket sized diary notebook. It's a $5\frac{3}{8}$" x $3\frac{5}{8}$" life saver. Everything I know is recorded in that tattered binder. Everything. Dates, addresses, phone numbers, sermon notes, quotes, 25 years of experiences, expense accounts. The little book is priceless. It is also a crutch.

Thus, on my approach to the Philadelphia airport when I reached into my pocket and found it gone...I went into Reaction. I last remembered having it in a phone booth at Washington National Airport. My whole world shuddered to a stop.

In the moments that followed I hit every possible emotion: despair, frustration, anger, hate self, hate God, hate National Airport, hate the phone company.

But Reaction lasted only one minute 48 seconds, and suddenly I was into Recovery—praising God. Not bad. Two years ago the nausea would have lasted three days.

"Okay, God," I said aloud, "I'm wiped out. Ground zero. All my good stuff is gone. Now it's just me and your Holy Spirit." The more I thought about that, the better it got. Until I was genuinely *glad* the stupid book was gone.

A week later, a little package arrived in the mail. Inside was my notebook. And a note.

Dear Mr. May:

We located this notebook at Gate 16 at Washington National Airport. After a glance at its contents I was sure it was a treasured article that must be returned promptly. I did a little checking and here you are.

Sincerely,
Bob Walters
Customer Services
Allegheny Airlines

P.S. As a deacon in the Christian church I know how much these things mean and I feel honored to be able to help a man of God like yourself!

Wow! From zero to full speed in five seconds.

"By the way, Sweetheart, I seem to have misplaced my pen."

# Unloading the Extra Weight

For some time I have suspected that "gaining weight" is contagious. This was never much of a problem while we were living in the jungles of South America. But here, in the United States, it's one of the most serious problems facing Christians.

In our household not only are the Mays constantly fighting the overweight syndrome, but our dog, cat, and even our canary have the problem.

Recently my airplane caught it also.

I could hardly believe it when the mechanic called from the hangar and said the crew weighed my plane and found it overweight. I questioned the accuracy of the scales. (Don't we always?) Jim assured me they weighed the airplane three times on two different sets of scales.

"You just have to face it, Bern. That plane has gained 200 pounds since it was manufactured in 1964."

Not only that, but no one knows where the extra weight came from. All we know is JAARS has a fat plane.

I should have known. The last time I took off with four persons, baggage, and full fuel we barely got off the ground. I blamed the poor performance on tired engines. They were tired all right—tired of pulling all that extra weight around.

We've been joking about having the only plane enrolled in Weight Watchers. But it's really a serious matter. Unless we can shed the extra weight, the plane's utility is seriously limited. In fact, it looks like surgery may be the only answer. But what do we amputate? The nose wheel? Maybe an extra wing since it has two any-way? Whatever, we just can't carry 200 extra pounds and have space for the cargo we need to deliver.

So, we're currently working on the problem. If we can figure out where the extra weight came from, maybe we can get rid of it.

The same is true with a friend of mine. Like my plane, he looks normal. But over the years he has picked up a heavy load of guilt. In fact, he now walks in a bent-over position. Amazing, how guilt hangs on and builds up!

The Apostle Paul, facing a long cross-country trek, rec-ognized the necessity of traveling light. Before takeoff, he said, "lay aside every weight" that prevents us from being airborne. In other words, if we are going to "mount up with wings as eagles" we're going to have to be spiritual weight watchers.

The flight is tough enough without carrying a lot of excess cargo.

# Landing in Troubled Waters

Landing a float plane in the flooded Amazon River is an exercise in judgment.

When the rains come during February and March, the river rises as much as 100 feet, overflowing its banks and flooding thousands of miles of jungle. As the water covers the land and finds its way back to the river, it picks up tons of debris—logs, bushes, whatever. It is not unusual to see whole trees floating down the Amazon, some with small animals still clinging to the branches for survival.

Finding a clear stretch of water in which to land a plane when the river is at flood stage is nearly impossible. What appears to be smooth water on the downwind leg can be a cluttered mess of floating trees and debris by the time you make your turn for final approach. It is a terrifying experience to find your runway—which moments before appeared clear—suddenly filled with bobbing trees and stumps.

Even when you identify a good spot for landing, you wonder if a submerged tree may be floating just below the surface. Planes have landed on what appeared to be smooth water, only to be destroyed by logs hidden in the muddy river. The pilot is always looking for some clue to hidden danger—a ripple in the water, a branch sticking up.

The greatest difficulty, though, is not with the river—but with the pilot himself.

Invariably as you turn final, all lined up for a landing, you spot another area of the river that looks better. The inexperienced pilot may change his mind and try to shift to the more appealing spot. Often when he gets closer, he sees something there he doesn't like and shifts back to his first choice. (There is nothing worse than being on final for two points.) The results are invariably embarrassing, sometimes disastrous.

The problem is focus. You have to make a decision and stay with it, keeping your objective clearly in focus.

Jesus said the Christian should learn to concentrate on doing one thing. It's not a sin to be a one-talent person. The sin lies in wanting to do ten things with your one talent and getting so frustrated that you wind up achieving nothing at all.

I've watched average pilots make excellent landings in troubled waters. The secret is landing on only one place at a time.

# Handling Failure

Often the way a man handles failure tells more about his character—and his ability—than the way he handles success.

As a check pilot my first assignment was to "check out" Eddie Lind as a pilot in the Norseman, a large, heavy floatplane of yesteryear. Eddie learned the aircraft systems well, and did a great job on the written test. I flew with him every day for a week, showing him how to handle the difficult landings and take-offs in the swirling, muddy rivers of the Amazon basin. The second week I flew as co-pilot, letting him take the controls. At the end of that time I reported to the chief pilot that he was ready.

"Has he made a bad landing yet?"

"No, every landing has been just right."

"Then he's not ready," he replied.

The chief pilot went on to explain to me that until a pilot has made a bad landing, he isn't ready to be a pilot-in-command.

"You need to find out how he handles the plane when things go wrong," he said. "Go back and fly with him until he makes a bad landing. See how he recovers. Then you'll know whether he's ready or not."

For two weeks more I rode as co-pilot, hoping for a bad landing. But Eddie was a great pilot. Every take-off and landing was near perfect.

Then it happened. We were making an approach to land at a river junction in the upper Amazon, near the village of Atalaya. The current was swift and a lot of debris was floating in the water. A brisk crosswind was blowing. The approach pattern was too tight and from my right seat I could see the indecision on Eddie's face. He wasn't sure just where to touch down in order to miss the passing logs in the river. It was going to be rough. I gritted my teeth and held on, determined to let him fly the plane without my help on the controls.

The plane hit hard, then bounced. One wing dropped low. Airspeed was falling off. Eddie pushed the controls forward and hit the throttle, gaining control just as we touched down again. It was a great recovery.

As soon as the plane was moored against the bank he apologized for the hard landing. He recognized his mistakes and was mortified that after a month of perfect landings, it looked like he had bombed out as a jungle pilot.

I patted his shoulder but denied myself (and him) the huge smile that was trying to explode all over my face. He thought he was a failure. He wasn't, and I told him why. Back at the hangar I took out his file, wrote up the whole incident, sealed it, and printed across the front one word.

"Ready."

# The Greatest Is the Least—On and Off the Ground

The other night Bernie Jr. stopped by the house, wanting to talk about a fellow who in the world's eyes "had it all, and was at the top of the heap."

"Man, this college professor has everything. Twenty-nine years old. He owns his own accounting firm with offices all over the east. He teaches just for the fun of it. He's a sharp dresser. Witty. He radiates success and he's filled with hints on how to get ahead in this world. Man, he has the class eating out of his hand.

"But as I left the room this afternoon," Bernie added, "I began to compare him with Leon Downs. I haven't been able to stop thinking about it."

Leon Downs! I thought.

Leon worked all his life on a shift at Sun Oil in Marcus Hook, Pennsylvania. He never finished high school. He had nothing. But after he retired he'd drive his battered old car down to Waxhaw, North Carolina, and stay with us for a few weeks at a time. He went around the JAARS Center mowing lawns and doing little odd jobs for those who didn't have any money.

Shortly before Leon died, Bernie had ridden down from Marcus Hook with him. Bernie had come in the house shaking his head.

"Boy, old Leon sure drives funny. He holds his head way back and you can't tell if maybe he's asleep or something. He drives real slow and people honk at him. And he wears that dumb old railroad hat all the time. I guess if you didn't know him you'd think he's one of those men who goes around picking up bottles all the time."

We chuckled about Leon, but there was something else about him. He was a man who lived in and for another kingdom. Unlike the young professor who was intent on getting all he could, Leon was interested in only one thing—giving. Everything.

"I think about him every time I pray," Bernie said quietly. "I try to imagine old Leon thinking about what he would do if he were rich, but I can't. Even though he had nothing, he always seemed to think he was the richest man in the world. All he ever wanted to do was help someone else."

There was a lull in the conversation, and things got real quiet. Outside I could hear the night sounds—the katydids and tree frogs.

"I've been doing a lot of thinking about great people," Bernie said. "I think about my professor. I think about you, Dad. I think about some of the missionaries I've known. But if I was truthful, I'd say Leon Downs was probably the greatest person I've ever met."

Bernie Jr. didn't say any more. But far off in the distance, out beyond the katydids, the tree frogs, beyond the stars all the way into eternity, I thought I could hear the faint sound of someone clapping.

# NECESSARY
# INSPECTIONS

# The Word of a Gauge

Jim Baptista is a detail man. Gripping a mental clipboard, he pores over every detail of pre-flight procedure before nosing his craft from terra firma.

One time I flew with him to Tucson, Arizona, to pick up a surplus DC-3 for JAARS. It looked like a good prospect and everything checked out as we took it down through the check list. Until we ran up the engines. Jim and I exchanged glances as a gauge showed the right-engine oil pressure was low. That's serious. We were certainly in no position to buy another engine so we did some checking.

The log book showed the engine was brand new. A further check showed the reason for changing the original engine was low oil pressure. It was rather difficult to accept that two engines, one of them new, could develop identical problems.

So the detail man decided to do a little experimenting. Crawling under the instrument panel, Jim reversed the lines on the oil gauges, attaching the right engine line to the left gauge and vice versa. You guessed it. Now the left engine showed low oil pressure. Conclusion: The gauge, not the engine, was at fault. Someone had installed a new, $12,000 engine because of a false reading on a $30 gauge.

For some reason, we habitually take the word of a gauge, simply because it appears before us on an instrument panel. A broken or malfunctioning oil pressure gauge, altimeter, or compass could cause a pilot to take drastic action—action that might even cost him his life.

As we flew home, those two big engines purring on each wing, I thought of other gauges which proclaim "truth." Some call for radical change. Others assure me that everything's okay.

Call me a spiritual "detail man" if you wish, but I wonder about some of those gauges. I've stopped taking the word of a gauge, even if it has always been right before. No gauge—no voice—gives a true reading all the time.

A gauge that's stuck in the green when the engine is going wild can be just as fatal as one that causes you to chop the throttle when nothing is wrong. The wise man reverses his lines now and then, checks the Manual...or even consults the Manufacturer.

Somewhere, sometime, it might save him a burn-out.

# Inspections

Every time a member of Wycliffe is elected or appointed to a new position, he is required to undergo a doctrinal examination. So it wasn't much of a shock when a bulky envelope from the secretary of the board landed on my desk after I was elected to the board of directors. The politely worded note inside requested me to reaffirm my original doctrinal position.

That's okay. It gave me the opportunity to plunge into the Word and carve out restatements of what I believe about God, God's Son, the Holy Spirit, the Bible, and other foundational truths.

About the same time I received a letter from my home church asking me to do the same for them. They've got a rule that all missionaries sponsored by the church should periodically be reviewed to make sure they haven't slipped into some form of false doctrine.

I joked with my wife that if I didn't know that the folks at Wycliffe and the officials in my home church loved me, I'd be feeling a little insecure with all these doctrinal examinations coming at me.

Inspections are a good thing. I've lived with them ever since I began in aviation. But as I penciled out the forms, I couldn't help thinking back to some things I'd been told about the aircraft inspections we conduct in our hangars at JAARS. We'd been giving our aircraft 100-hour inspections—a pretty sacred procedure among mechanics. But then someone got the idea to inspect our inspections. The results were painful. We found that our mechanics were spending a lot of time and energy inspecting the wrong things. We'd been extremely thorough—but thorough in the extreme.

Some parts were meticulously over-inspected while others went totally ignored. For instance, our crew religiously undid a hundred screws in the wing during each 100-hour inspection to look at the spar. *A spar wouldn't change in a hundred years of constant flight!* At the same time, we gave little or no attention to things like small rubber hoses or instrument air filters—things which deteriorate constantly and give us chronic problems.

We wore out our airplanes and mechanics with inspections, consuming time and energy on relatively unimportant matters while we blissfully ignored those items which needed our constant attention.

I don't mind inspections. But I get concerned when I'm checked for the wrong things. Not once has anyone checked me out on John 17, and how well I'm doing with Jesus' prayer "that they all might be one." At every investigation someone takes off my inspection plate and examines my wing spar of biblical inspiration, but no one ever checks my filters to find out if I'm so clogged up with unforgiveness and bitterness that love can't flow through. God has a different perspective...a different checklist. The Bible tells me that even if I leave everything behind, go off to some distant mission field, spend 60 years uttering doctrinally precise words—even giving my body to be burned and have not love....

Inspections are good. All of us need them.

If the right things get inspected.

By the right inspector.

I'm convinced the Master Designer who put us together

is eager to maintain His high performance standards. If we'll only let Him.

# Go, No Go

Every airline has a "go, no go" list comprising a combination of weather factors, mechanical checklists, and the pilot's own cockpit checklist.

Example: A malfunctioning instrument, a badly frayed seatbelt, or a tornado at the end of the runway means a "no go." On the other hand, a burned out light bulb in the instrument panel, worn tires, or just dirt and bugs on the windshield are acceptable problems; the pilot gets a "go"—he can take off.

When the chief pilots from all our overseas operations got together for a flight safety seminar, I began to realize that even "acceptable" problems can kindle a disaster if they are not handled correctly. When the pressure is on and the weather is bad, some small discrepancy hardly noticed on takeoff can loom suddenly like a vengeful giant. Just before a spectacular air-to-air collision, one airline pilot reported that there were so many bugs splattered on the windshield he could barely see through it. It was his last report.

We were just about through the safety session when one seasoned aviator spoke up and grounded us all.

"Frankly, gentlemen," he said, "it's not the discrepancies in the airplane that bother me as much as the discrepancies in the pilot. When I'm in the air with things inside me that I know aren't right—I become the hazard."

You won't find it in a pre-flight instruction manual—but he's right. Who wants to fly with a pilot who's just had a bitter argument with his wife...or who is seething underneath at his copilot...or who has an uncontrollable temper...or who is so filled with pride and self-righteousness that he refuses to listen to correction?

Bugs on the windshield. Nothing so urgent as a faulty fuel line or plunging oil pressure—just a little compromise with clear vision. Little things. Like petty jealousy, impatience, prejudice, careless words, prayerless mornings, impure thoughts. In an aircraft it's the little things which, in a crisis, could mean the difference between life or death. For the believer, bugs on the windshield could rob visibility at a critical moment of decision resulting in moral disaster or irreparable loss of witness.

Every Christian leader, parent, or preacher needs to have his own "go, no go" list before he straps himself into a place of responsibility. When the going gets rough, everything better be up to specs.

# Cleaning the Connections

It was a dark and stormy night.

It really was. One of my closest friends is a professional writer who laughs at people like me who start a story that way. But when you're trying to make an instrument landing with a vintage DC-3 on an island in the West Indies with your ADF (automatic direction finder) out of whack—and it's a dark and stormy night—what else can you say? I can assure you it was no laughing matter.

That night as I approached Kingston, Jamaica, in a screaming gale, my ADF chose to rebel. It pointed straight ahead for a while. Then it pointed over toward Spain. At one point it aimed to the rear. Fortunately, I had dual ADFs on the plane; the second one remained loyal and I landed safely.

Later, I watched the radio repairman troubleshoot the

faulty radio. After a few simple checks, he turned and said, "You'll never keep it on course with a bad connection, Captain. The problem is in this cannon plug."

I watched as he disassembled the complicated plug with 20 pins which fit neatly into a 20-pin receptacle. Moisture in the connections had caused corrosion to build up on the contacts. The unwanted resistance in the wires resulted in an unreliable ADF.

Besides getting an instrument repaired, I got some good advice. "Every so often, Captain," he remarked, "you need to stop and clean up your connections."

The phrase repeated itself recently on an inner speaker when our family went on a vacation to the beach.

There is nothing like five people in a crowded camper to test the condition of your wiring. At the end of the first day it was apparent that we had some fragile connections. The best communication we could manage was a lot of harsh static. My wife threatened to go home. My oldest son, a high school senior, took courage in the fact that this would be his last family vacation.

We couldn't even agree on what kind of soda pop to drink.

The next morning I decided we had to clean up some connections. We examined ourselves—each one in relation to the others. We found that parents aren't always fair and that resentments build up between brothers. We leveled with each other, confessed, prayed, cleaned up the connections, and went on to have one of our best family vacations ever.

Now I'm thinking I need to check on some of my other connections. How about those with my fellow missionaries? Or my neighbors? Or my relatives?

If I'm going to stay on course and be effective in my work and ministry, I'm going to have to keep the connections clean—because for sure, there will be some more dark and stormy nights.

# Are Your Tanks Full?

Making assumptions is dangerous—especially when it comes to the assumption that airplane fuel tanks are fully loaded before takeoff.

Some years ago in Ecuador, a four-engine DC-4 developed trouble after takeoff. Ten minutes after getting airborne, the pilot of the heavily-loaded cargo plane radioed back to Guayaquil that one of his engines had failed. Calmly he advised that he had feathered the engine and was proceeding on course.

Three minutes later he radioed again that the second engine had quit. He was returning to the airport. A minute later he called frantically. Engines three and four had also failed and he was going down. Miraculously, he landed the big plane in a banana patch and all three crew members climbed out without a scratch.

An investigation revealed that each crew member thought the other had fueled the aircraft. As a result, they had taken off with empty tanks. One minute everything sounded great. The next, they were headed to earth. A DC-4 doesn't glide very far without power.

The punch line: the out-of-gas plane was loaded with barrels of aviation fuel to be delivered to another airport.

Just such an oversight in the spiritual area came into view recently when we dined with a president of a Christian college. The conversation drifted from our national plight, to the moral decline, to the breakdown of the family, and then to this startler.

The college chaplain, concerned about the lack of spiritual depth among the students, devised a simple test of Bible knowledge. No tricky questions, just a straightforward attempt to see how much of the Bible they had in them. Get ready for the result. Although 95 percent of those quizzed were from Christian homes and evangelical churches, they were biblically illiterate. Almost none of them knew the number of books in the Bible. Some thought Moses was a disciple of Jesus, and the majority said Exodus was in the New Testament.

The danger, of course, is they all think they're running on a full tank. They believe they have something that in reality isn't there.

I rejoice when I hear 35 percent of the population is born again. I'm glad everyone is getting airborne for God. I only hope, before taking off over some dense jungle, they check their tanks. Remember, even after three years of Bible school, Jesus still told His disciples not to witness until they had tarried in an upper room for spiritual power.

An airplane crash, you know, can ruin your whole day.

# INVOLVEMENT WITH THE FLIGHT PLAN

# Caring Enough to Cry

Last week in my office, in the middle of a meeting with three businessmen, I began to cry. I still get embarrassed thinking about it.

A contractor from Philadelphia had flown down to spend the day at the JAARS Center here in Waxhaw. With him were two business friends who are interested in missions. We ate lunch, toured the Center, and then returned to my office. Pulling out a file, I began reading to them excerpts from cases illustrating JAARS' involvement in recent mercy flights: a snakebite victim to the hospital in Peru...a doctor to an Indian village in Ecuador to stop an epidemic...relief to landslide victims in Colombia.

Then I came across the case of an Indian girl named Rita in western Brazil. That touched it off. I still don't know what happened to me, but all of a sudden I began to weep. All choked up, I blushed like a schoolgirl. Fortunately, my business friends were very kind. They didn't laugh. I quickly changed the subject to aircraft operating costs, fuel consumption, range, engine overhaul time, and other safe subjects in which we were interested.

I don't know—maybe they would have cried, too, if they'd known more about Rita. She'd been carried in from the jungle to the home of two single women Wycliffe translators. The moment they saw her they knew she could not live without prompt medical attention. One, a nurse, examined Rita. Finding her to be severely anemic, desperately ill with malaria, and five months pregnant, she sent a radio message to the center at Porto Velho, requesting an emergency flight.

A pilot and an aviation mechanic flew out in a Cessna

206 and soon Rita was in the maternity hospital in Porto Velho. The doctors discovered her system was laced with deadly parasites and the battle was on to save her life. Men and women at the Wycliffe Center put aside busy schedules to provide around-the-clock nursing care. Many gave blood. When Rita experienced a severe reaction to a blood transfusion and the doctors said she was dying, everyone at the Center dropped what they were doing and gathered for prayer. Once again her life was spared. The hospital staff expressed amazement that so many people could love one poor, illiterate Indian woman.

I can't tell you why I cried over the report. Maybe it was the fact that Rita was so remote in that endless jungle, seemingly without help. Maybe it was because all JAARS had to do was send a plane and fly her to a hospital. Or it may have been the expense. The flight which saved Rita's life cost only $62.10. Or perhaps it was the fact that she accepted Christ in the hospital and went back not only healed, but transformed. I don't know. But something got to me and suddenly I began to cry right in front of those businessmen.

But then...why should I be ashamed to cry? Jesus wept. Nehemiah cried when he heard the report on the sad state of Jerusalem. And the reports I'm getting from around the world are certainly every bit as grim. God said we should go forth weeping if we are to be productive for Him. Our Lord is looking for men who care enough to cry.

If we don't, who will?

# Of Thermostats and Thermometers

Recently Dave Wike, Eastern Airline pilot, and I were flying a JAARS Helio down V-93 en route from Hampton, New Hampshire, to Philadelphia. The weather was marginal. Freezing level was 8,000 feet, right where we had been cleared to fly.

As Dave flew I kept my eye on the outside air temperature (OAT) gauge—which is nothing more than an old-fashioned thermometer. A change of one or two degrees could mean the difference between wings and prop covered with ice or smooth sailing.

As the ice began to build up I reached for the mike and requested a change of altitude from New York Center. Another five minutes at 8,000 feet would have been disastrous.

"What we need," I shouted to Dave as we dropped down to warmer air at 6,000 feet, "is a thermostat out there, not just a thermometer."

Thermometers measure the environment. Thermostats change it. Our house has a thermostat. It measures, reacts, and brings change. It makes our house comfortable.

There seem to be a lot of thermometers in the Kingdom these days. It's easy to get a reading on everything from the Charismatics to the Catholics. Everyone seems to have an opinion. Sometimes I think the church is in danger of paralysis by analysis.

Rare are the thermostat people. Those who are not content with simply measuring, but are in the business of bringing change. Those who can cool down an explosive situation or build a fire under a cold church.

Recently a nearby church renovated its building. When they put up the new steeple they left off the cross and installed a weathervane. Weathervanes, like thermometers, only measure the environment. Crosses change things.

There is nothing wrong with measuring and evaluating. Every thermostat has a built-in thermometer. But the need in the Kingdom today is for men who will do more than analyze. The cry is for men who will take an uncomfortable situation and change it to meet needs and glorify God.

Otherwise, we have no choice but to request a change of flight plan to a lower altitude. And that's no way to climb on course!

# The Final Banquet

In early May, 1972, my good friend Bengt Junvik became the object of a massive search and rescue operation while ferrying a new plane to Galena, Alaska. The confusing Rainy Pass, a swinging compass, and a mountain wave depression resulted in a crash in an inaccessible mountain canyon. Bengt survived the crash unhurt, but was hopelessly lost. For the next four days a blizzard blanketed the whole area.

Meanwhile friends and officials were doing all they could. Fifty search and rescue teams, and as many civilian and military aircraft scanned the mountains. A business friend in California went to Alaska and hired extra planes and helicopters to help in the hunt. Christian friends around the world prayed.

On the fifth day search planes flew right above Bengt, but they didn't see him. By the thirteenth day the search planes had given up. His supplies depleted, he considered his condition beyond hope. But on that thirteenth day a helicopter came down the canyon and spotted him.

The lost was found! You can imagine the exultation.

His wife and children, his friends, the search teams, everyone shouted for joy.

A banquet was ordered. The largest place available, which could seat 250 people, was packed to the doors. Emceeing was the businessman who had engaged the helicopter after all the other planes had given up. Bengt himself had the opportunity to say "thank you" to the men who had spent hours and days searching for him, a lost man they didn't know.

As Bengt related this story to me, I couldn't help thinking of another banquet. Jesus will be the Master of ceremonies. The great Banquet Hall will be filled. I can hear tribesmen—Campas, Kewas, Aucas—saying "Thank you for searching, thank you for organizing the rescue team, thank you for staying with it. Because you cared, we're here."

Won't that be great? This is what JAARS is all about. A search and rescue team for the tribes still lost.